BOOK 3

Especially in *Jazzy Style*

7 Stylized Solos for Late Intermediate Pianists

Dennis Alexander

I have always loved improvising at the piano, and I am so fortunate that my piano teachers I studied with as a child never discouraged me from doing this! I worked my way through college by playing in a private dinner club every weekend for almost four years. It was then that I really learned to appreciate and experiment with jazz styles.

I've always felt that classically trained pianists would play music by the master composers even better if they had the ability to improvise and/or perform music by some of the jazz greats such as Oscar Peterson and George Shearing. Young pianists today can benefit so much from the syncopated rhythms of jazz, the unique and often unexpected harmonies, and the freedom of expression inherent in this style.

In *Especially in Jazzy Style, Book 3*, students will be motivated by the infectious rhythms, harmonies, and lyrical melodies found in the pieces. Teachers will have fun sharing the challenges of jazz styles with students who might be playing this type of music for the very first time. Enjoy, and be inspired by your personal interpretation of the solos in this collection.

Dennis Alexander

Copyright © MMX by Alfred Music Publishing Co., Inc.
All Rights Reserved.   Printed in USA.
ISBN-10: 0-7390-7065-7
ISBN-13: 978-0-7390-7065-9

Contents printed on 100% recycled paper.

Barclay Street Blues

Dennis Alexander

4

Porto Alegre

Dennis Alexander

Always and Forever

Dennis Alexander

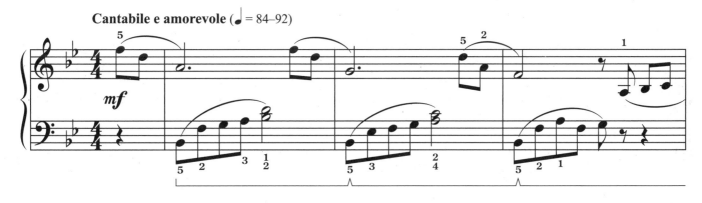

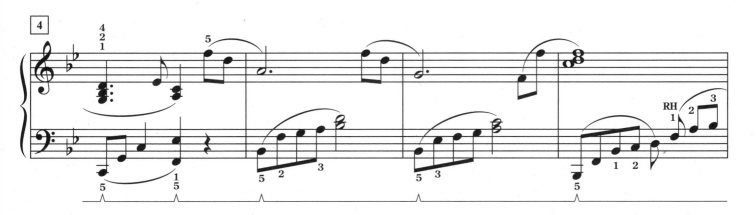

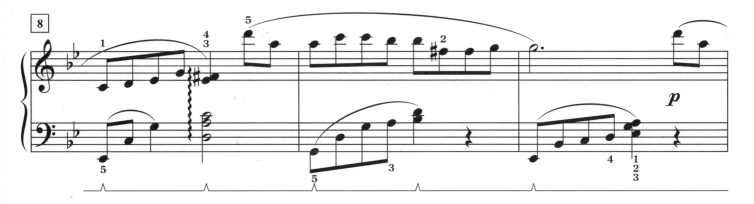

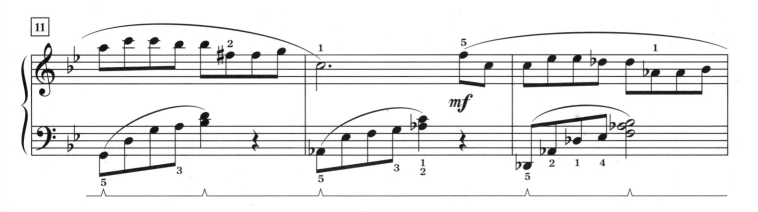

10

11

A Million Miles Away

Dennis Alexander

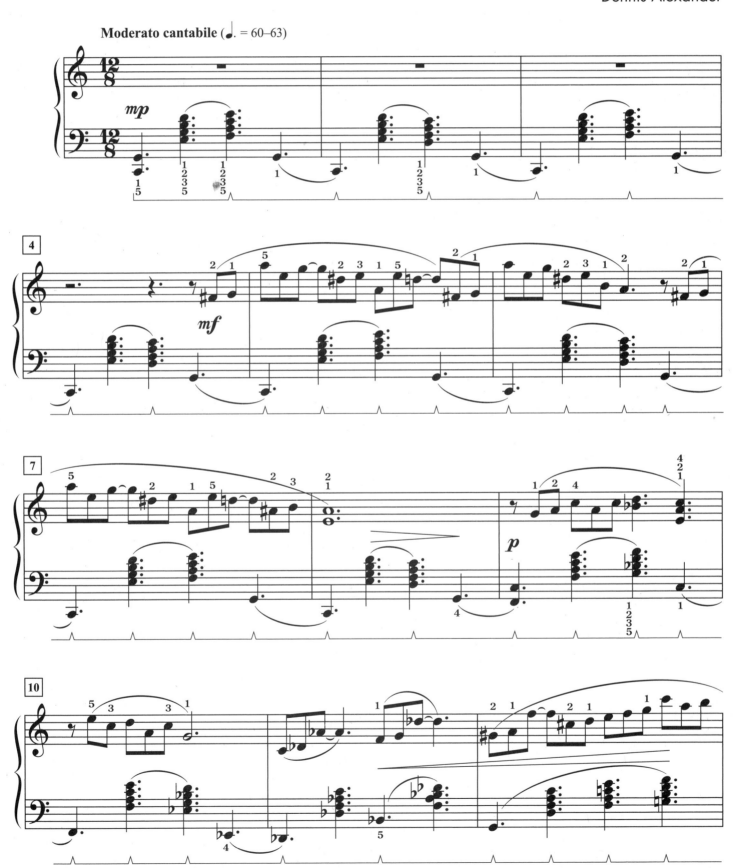

14

Double Duty

Dennis Alexander

16

In My Own Space

Dennis Alexander

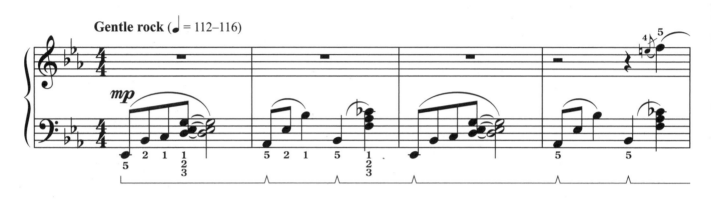

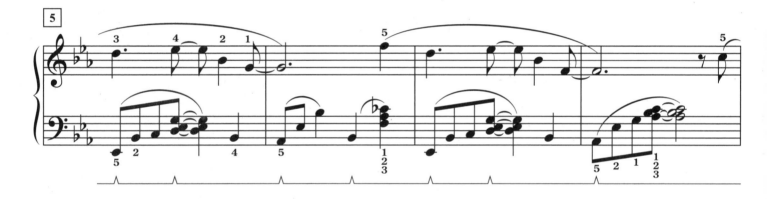

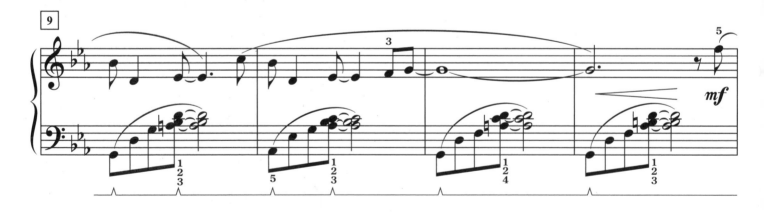

Jazz at Five

Dennis Alexander